A heartfelt thanks for your support!
Most often it is not easy working with our own children at home, and its far less easy to work on math with them.
With my own children, I struggled and made many mistakes, but I've come to understand that I needed those struggles to create, develop and provide you with this book that will make the road to mental math mastery smoother for your family.
I thank dedicated parents and educators for putting in that extra effort in fostering a strong math foundation in your young ones. And I am truly thankful to you for trying my unique approach to developing mental math mastery.
And don't forget, your young ones are capable for much more challenging math then they are expected to accomplish in any American daycare or pre-k.

- Dr. Ameerah Anakaona -

Welcome Mathematician Families!

Dear Math-Minded Families,

Thank you and congratulations for taking this step towards investing in math mastery for your child(ren). For many, abacus-based math instruction is a new way of approaching math. With that in mind, I have designed a very fun and user-friendly system for families new to the abacus. **I strongly encourage you to purchase the jr.counter to get the most of this book.**

This system includes:

- Introduction to the abacus using a simplified abacus, the jr.counter
- Counting
- Positioning
- Adding /subtracting
- Journaling
- Mental Practice, and
- Word problems (with an emphasis on great historical figures)

You will find that using the Mathematician, Jr. system will significantly develop and improve not only your child's ability to understand the fundamentals of math language and number relationships but additionally, your child will have enhanced mental capabilities. Lastly, children will be able to better explain how he/she has derived at their answer.

To help you commit to increased math learning, it would be a great idea to add an incentive to the contract on the next page and have all parties sign. This contract will help keep your child motivated to complete their Mathematician, Jr. level I book.

Please follow the proposed progress, complete at least 10 problems per day, and trust in the process.

If at any time you need additional tools or support contact **ameerah@mathjr.org** or **www.mathjr.org**.

Use the contract on the next page: make signing the contract a fun and formal event!

Kids need to be taught that with hard work comes great rewards, introduce them to the contract and discuss the reward that they will receive once they successfully complete their Mathematician, Jr. Workbook.

The Mathematician's Contract

The Mathematician's Contract

I, _____ (the Mathematician, Jr.) commit to practicing at least 10 problems per day so I can become and Mathematician, Jr. I will work in a place where I can focus and I will allow myself to struggle a little while trying to figure out the answer on my own before asking for help.

I will also be sure to focus very hard when it comes to the mental math practice pages.

_____   _____
Future Mathematician, Jr.   Date

_____   _____
Parent/Witness   Date

The Mathematician's Parent Contract

After _____ (Mathematician's name) successfully completes Mathematician Workbook Level I, I _____ (Parent/guardian) pledge to (reward your child will receive for successful completion of this book)

_____
_____
_____
_____

_____   _____
Future Mathematician, Jr.   Date

_____   _____
Parent/Witness   Date

READY, SET...
INTRODUCE THE JR.COUNTER

Introducing your child to a new skill is an exciting time. In this case it serves as the gateway to young children engaging with math in a fun and meaningful way. This will be the one of the few activities that your child will develop both the left and right sides of their brain simultaneously.

Here are some suggestions to help make this introduction fun and meaningful.

I. Make it special:

   a. Let you Math Jr. know that not many children in this country use a jr.counter and it's a very special type of skill for them to learn

   b. Help them feel special for taking on this challenge!

II. Before you begin, have your Math Jr. guess what the jr.counter is used for.

   a. Give your child the jr.counter and have them tell you what they think it is for.

   b. Don't discourage any silly responses, and laugh if it is funny.

   c. Compliment insightful and creative responses.

III. Have your Math Jr. try to figure out how to count with the jr.counter.

   a. Demonstrate how to count to ② (see page_____), and see if he/she can count to ③ based on your demonstration.

IV. Show your Math Jr. pictures or videos of other Math Jrs using their jr.counters, on an abacus or even doing mental math

   a. Use encouraging language: **"you'll be doing math like that soon"** or **"I know you are capable of doing math like that little girl/boy."**

How to use this book

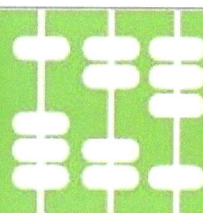

...introduces a new skill.

...tells you CAN use your jr.counter to calculate the problem set.

...tells you that you CAN'T USE your jr.counter to calculate the problem set. You must 'imagine' that you are moving your counter with your hand

...shows that you must complete problems that are 'DICTACTED TO YOU.' Which means that you will not see the problems on paper. You will hear the problems and have calculate. YOU CAN USE YOUR COUNTER WITH DICATIONTION.

...shows you when it's time to journal about what you've learned. Explaining your math is very important.

...when you see this icon, its time for you to put away your jr.counter and imagine yourself moving it with your hand to help you solve the math.

...this icon signals that it's time to use your jr.counter to complete a word problem. You'll be guided with steps to help you figure out what the problem is asking and how to answer it correctly.

...represents an assessment or a test. This page will measure how much you have learned for a particular lesson.
Try your best!

Learn the parts and positions of the jr.counter

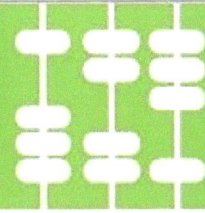

Jr. Counter

Introducing your Jr. Counter: The Jr. Counter is a simplified version of the traditional and ancient Japanese Soroban abacus. It has a few key parts to make counting, adding, and subtraction easy:

1. **The upper 5 bead**
2. **The lower beads**
3. **The answer rod**

The Jr. Counter's parts

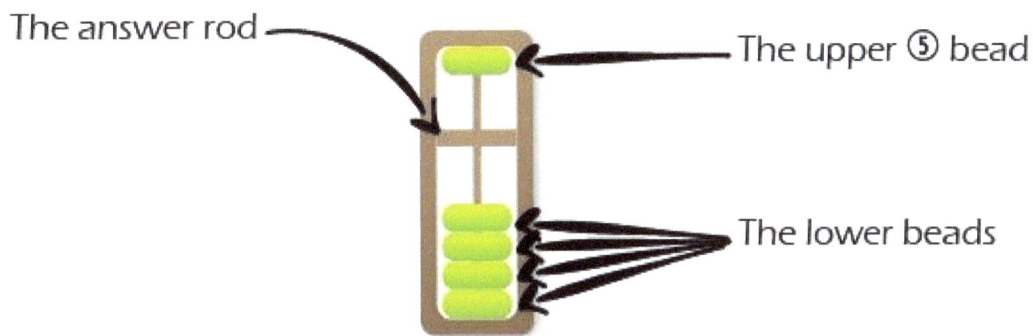

The answer rod

The upper ⑤ bead

The lower beads

Now You Try — Name the parts of the jr.counter

This is the

....

*Hint: if a bead is touching this, it gets counted.

This is the

....

*Hint: this bead has a higher number them the other ones.

These are the

....

*Hint: they are below the bead above.

The jr.counter's positions

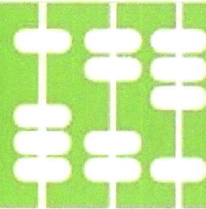

Jr. Counter

There are also **2** key positions that you'll need to know:
1. **The answer position**
2. **The zero-reset position**

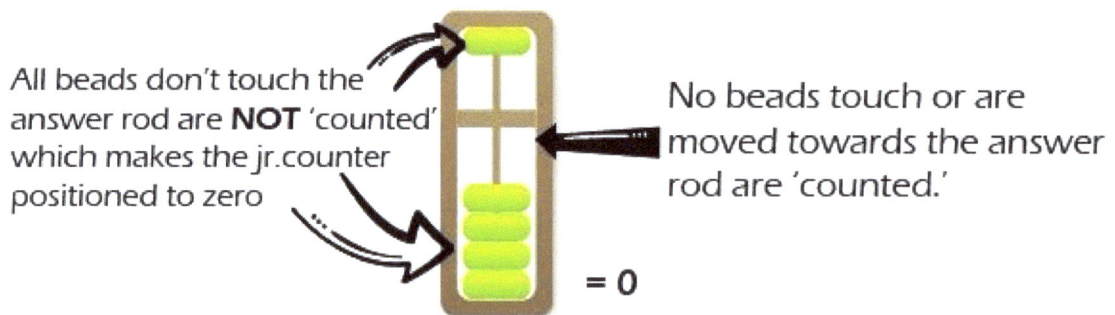

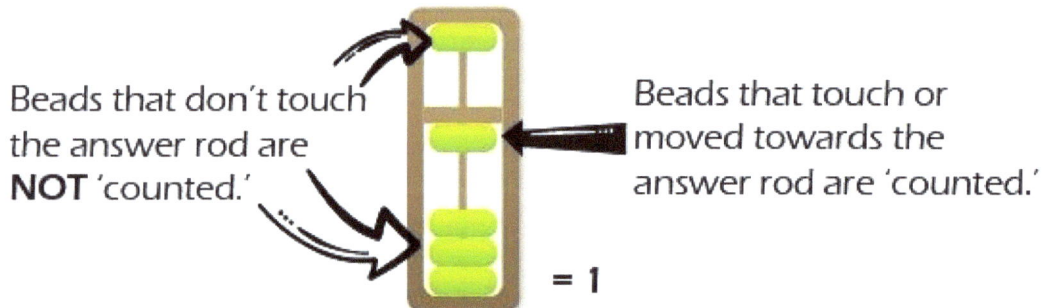

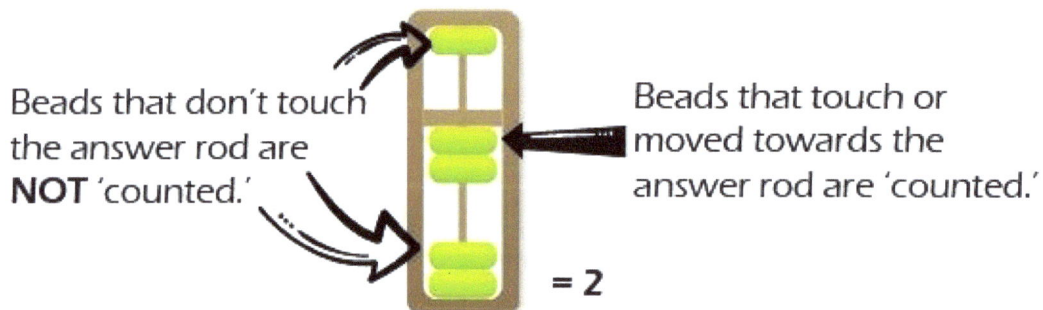

All beads don't touch the answer rod are **NOT** 'counted' which makes the jr.counter positioned to zero

No beads touch or are moved towards the answer rod are 'counted.'

= 0

Beads that don't touch the answer rod are **NOT** 'counted.'

Beads that touch or moved towards the answer rod are 'counted.'

= 1

Beads that don't touch the answer rod are **NOT** 'counted.'

Beads that touch or moved towards the answer rod are 'counted.'

= 2

The jr.counter's positions

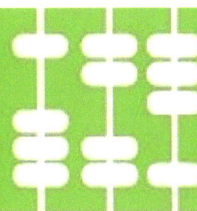

Beads that don't touch the answer rod are **NOT** 'counted.'

Beads that touch or moved towards the answer rod are 'counted.'

= 3

Beads that don't touch the answer rod are **NOT** 'counted.'

Beads that touch or moved towards the answer rod are 'counted.'

= 4

Bonus

Beads that touch or moved towards the answer rod are 'counted.'

Beads that don't touch the answer rod are **NOT** 'counted.'

= 5

*Counting, adding and subtracting to ⑤ is the next level skill. This example is just a brief introduction to mathematicians who may be grasping skills more quickly.

Practice Skill 1 (Positioning 0 to 4)

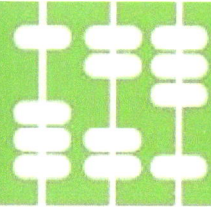

Directions: write what number is the jr.counter positioned?

1 ....

Directions: Draw in the beads on the jr.counter showing the number presented below.

(4) (1) (2) (3) (4)

In order to position my jr.counter to ① correctly, I need to:

....
....
....

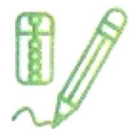

WORD BANK

Upper bead	one	add	zero	bead
Lower bead	move	substract	base position	two
Answer beam	push	take away	Jr. Counter	three

Practice Skill 1 (Positioning 0 to 4)

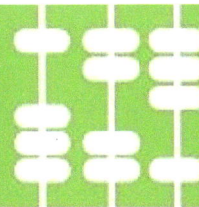

Directions: Draw in the beads on the jr.counter showing the number presented below.

3

1

3

0

2

4

In order to position my jr.counter to ② correctly, I need to (use first, next or lastly):

....

....

....

WORD BANK

Upper bead	one	add	zero	four
Lower bead	move	substract	base position	two
Answer beam	push	take away	Jr. Counter	three

www.mathjr.org

First, set your Jr. Counter to the ZERO-RESET position. (no beads are touching the ANSWER-ROD)

0 =

Next, to count to ① move the top lower bead up towards the ANSWER-ROD

1 =

To count to ② move the NEXT lower bead up towards the ANSWER-ROD so that it touches the first bead.

2 =

To count to ③ move the NEXT lower bead up towards the ANSWER-ROD so that it touches the second bead.

3 =

To count to ④ move the NEXT lower bead up towards the ANSWER-ROD so that it touches the third bead.

= 4

New Skill 2 - Counting UP

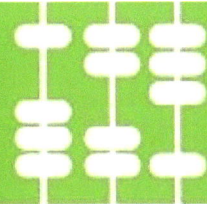

Counting up by ①   Counting up by ②   Counting up by ③   Counting up by ④

Starting with ⓪, every time you move **ANY LOWER** bead towards the answer rod, you count up.

You can count up from any bead, as long as you move a bead towards the answer rod, you are counting

When you count up a bead from ②, you add to the value.

You can count UP starting with ANY BEAD

Starting with ①   You can count up by ②

Starting with ②   You can count up by ①

Directions: Count UP by ② and draw in the beads to show your answer.

New Skill 2 - Counting UP

Counting up by ①   Counting up by ②   Counting up by ③   Counting up by ④

Starting with ⓪, every time you move **ANY LOWER** bead towards the answer rod, you count up.

You can count up from any bead, as long as you move a bead towards the answer rod, you are counting

When you count up a bead from ②, you add to the value.

You can count UP starting with ANY BEAD

Starting with ①   You can count up by ②

Starting with ②   You can count up by ①

Directions: Count UP by ② and draw in the beads to show your answer.

www.mathjr.org

Practice Skill 2 - Counting DOWN

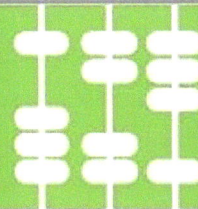

Learn how to count DOWN: 4 - 3 - 2 - 1 - 0

Starting with ④, every time you move a bead AWAY FROM the answer rod, you count up.

You can count down from any bead, as long as your move a bead AWAY FROM the answer rod.

When you count DOWN from ②, you SUBTRACT or MOVE BEADS AWAY FROM the answer beam to

When you count DOWN from ①, you SUBTRACT or MOVE the last bead AWAY FROM the answer rod.

Once your jr.counter is at the zero-reset position you cannot count DOWN anymore.

You can count DOWN starting with ANY BEAD

Starting with ③   You can count down by ②

Starting with ②   You can count down by ②

Directions: Count DOWN by ① and draw in the beads to show your answer.

Practice Skill 2 - Counting DOWN

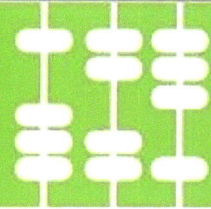

From the ④ position

count down by ①

....

count down by ③

....

count down by ②

....

count down by ⓪

....

count down by ④

....

From the ③ position

count down by ②

....

count down by ③

....

count down by ⓪

....

count down by ①

....

count down by ②

....

From the ② position

count down by ⓪

....

count down by ②

....

count down by ⓪

....

count down by ①

....

count down by ①

....

New Skill 3 - Adding 0-4 to 0

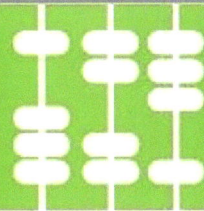

Instructions: To add a number on your Jr. Counter, you must push the bead towards the ANSWER-ROD. JUST LIKE COUNTING!

Example
1 + 0

To add ① on your Jr. Counter, move the top lower bead up towards the ANSWER-ROD

Example
2 + 0

To add ② to your Jr. Counter move the NEXT lower bead up towards the ANSWER-ROD so that it touches the first bead.

To add ③ on your Jr. Counter, move the NEXT lower bead up towards the ANSWER-ROD so that it touches the second bead.

Example
3 + 0

To add ④ move the NEXT lower bead up towards the ANSWER-ROD so that it touches the third bead.

Example
4 + 0

IT'S ALL the SAME

The same rules apply for adding 1, 2, 3 or 4 to any number. Just move the number of beads you are adding up towards the answer beam. 1+1, you just push the next bead from the resting position up to the answer beam.

Instructions: Here are some examples of how to add numbers ①, ②, ③, and ④ to zero using your jr.counter.

$1 + 0 = \ldots\ldots$

This jr.counter is in the zero position

+1
Add 1

Slide 1 lower bead up to add ①

$2 + 0 = \ldots\ldots$

This jr.counter is in the zero position

+2
Add 2

Slide 2 lower bead up to add ②

$3 + 0 = \ldots\ldots$

This jr.counter is in the zero position

+3
Add 3

Slide 3 lower bead up to add ③

$4 + 0 = \ldots\ldots$

This jr.counter is in the zero position

+4
Add 4

Slide 4 lower bead up to add ④

Draw the correct number of beads

Practice Skill 3 - Adding 0-4 to 0

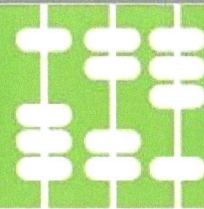

Directions: Use your jr.counter to add the following problems.

0	0	0	0	0	0	0	0	0	0
$^+1$	$^+2$	$^+3$	$^+4$	$^+4$	$^+3$	$^+2$	$^+1$	$^+0$	$^+3$
1	......	......	......	......	......	......	......	......	......

In order to add the number ② to ① correctly on my jr.counter, I need to:

....

....

....

WORD BANK

Upper bead	one	add	zero	bead
Lower bead	move	substract	base position	two
Answer beam	push	take away	Jr. Counter	three

Directions: Don't use your jr.counter, just the images provided, to calculate the following problems.

$^+1$	$^+2$	$^+3$	$^+4$	$^+4$	$^+3$	$^+2$	$^+1$	$^+0$	$^+3$
1	......	......	......	......	......	......	......	......	......

New Skill 3 - Adding 0-4

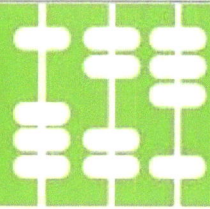

Instructions: Here are some examples of how to add numbers ①, ②, ③, and ④ using your jr.counter.

$$1 + 1 = 2$$

This jr.counter is in the one position

+1
Add 1

Slide 1 lower bead up to add ①

$$1 + 2 = 3$$

This jr.counter is in the one position

+2
Add 2

Slide 2 lower bead up to add ②

$$2 + 1 = 3$$

This jr.counter is in the two position

+1
Add 1

Slide 1 lower bead up to add ①

$$3 + 1 = 4$$

This jr.counter is in the three position

+1
Add 1

Slide 1 lower bead up to add ①

Practice Skill 3 - Adding 0-4

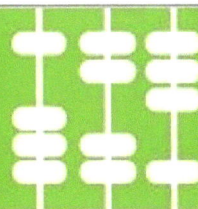

Directions: Don't use your jr.counter, just the images provided, to calculate the following problems.

$^+0$	$^+2$	$^+0$	$^+1$	$^+2$	$^+1$	$^+2$	$^+0$	$^+2$	$^+1$
1	......	......	......	......	......	......	......	......	......

Problem

Mary Bowser had 4 letters hidden in her secret pocket. She was able to give all 4 away. How many letters does she have left?

Step 1:
figure out what's being added or taken away in the problem

Step 2:
write your number sentence to show what's being added or taken away

your number sentence

....

Step 3:
write your answer

....

Here is your first word problem! Word problems are a really fun way to learn math and about some pretty amazing people in history. Check out the back of the book for more facts and questions about each Super-Person.

New Skill 4 - Adding 0 to 1-4

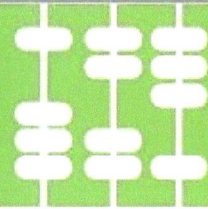

Instructions: To add a number on your Jr. Counter, you must push the bead towards the ANSWER-ROD. JUST LIKE COUNTING!

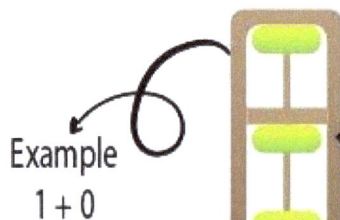

Example
1 + 0

To add ① on your Jr. Counter, move the top lower bead up towards the ANSWER-ROD

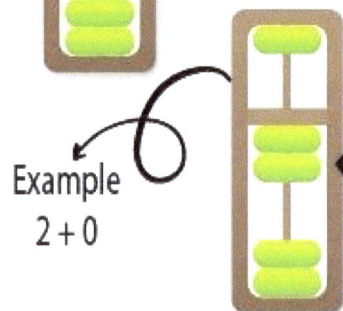

To add ② to your Jr. Counter move the NEXT lower bead up towards the ANSWER-ROD so that it touches the first bead.

Example
2 + 0

To add ③ on your Jr. Counter, move the NEXT lower bead up towards the ANSWER-ROD so that it touches the second bead.

Example
3 + 0

To add ④ move the NEXT lower bead up towards the ANSWER-ROD so that it touches the third bead.

Example
4 + 0

IT's ALL the SAME

The same rules apply for adding 1, 2,3 or 4 to any number. Just move the number of beads you are adding up towards the answer beam. 1+1, you just push the next bead from the resting position up to the answer beam.

New Skill 4 - Adding 0 to 0-4

Instructions: Here are some examples of how to add zero to numbers ①, ②, ③ and ④ using your jr.counter.

$1 + 0 = \ldots\ldots$

Put your jr.counter in the 1 position

Don't move any beads to add 0

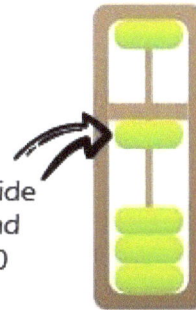

Don't slide any bead to add 0

$2 + 0 = \ldots\ldots$

Put your jr.counter in the 2 position

Don't move any beads to add 0

Don't slide any bead to add 0

$3 + 0 = \ldots\ldots$

Put your jr.counter in the 3 position

Don't move any beads to add 0

Don't slide any bead to add 0

$4 + 0 = \ldots\ldots$

Put your jr.counter in the 4 position

Don't move any beads to add 0

Don't slide any bead to add 0

Draw the correct number of beads

Practice Skill 4 - Adding 0-4

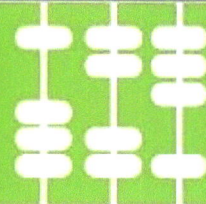

1	2	3	4	4	3	2	1	0	3
$^+0$	$^+0$	$^+0$	$^+0$	$^+0$	$^+0$	$^+0$	$^+0$	$^+0$	$^+0$
1	......	......	......	......	......	......	......	......	......

In order to add to zero correctly on my jr.counter, I need to:

....

....

$^+0$	$^+3$	$^+4$	$^+0$	$^+0$	$^+4$	$^+3$	$^+0$	$^+0$	$^+1$
1	......	......	......	......	......	......	......	......	......

Problem

Robert Smalls had **ZERO** naval ships to help his family. Then one day he got 3 naval ships. How many naval ships did he have in total?

Step 1:
figure out what's being added or taken away in the problem

Step 2:
write your number sentence to show what's being added or taken away

your number sentence

....

Step 3:
write your answer

....

Practice Skill 4 - Adding 0-4

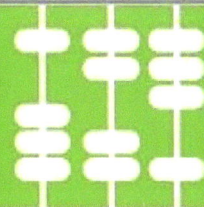

4	3	2	1	0	0	0	0	0	0
+ 0	+ 0	+ 0	+ 0	+ 0	+ 4	+ 1	+ 2	+ 3	+ 4
4	......	......	......	......	......	......	......	......	......

Problem

Harriet Tubman was following the North Star and had **3** people with her. At the firs stop, she added **zero** people, (it was too dangerous). How many people did she end up with?

Step 1:
figure out what's being added or taken away in the problem

Step 2:
write your number sentence to show what's being added or taken away

your number sentence

....

Step 3:
write your answer

....

+ 4	+ 1	+ 0	+ 1	+ 3	+ 0	+ 1	+ 3	+ 1	+ 1
4	......	......	......	......	......	......	......	......	......

Explain how to complete the following calculation: 0+2 (using: first, second, next and last) : ....
....

New Skill 5 - Subtracting 0-4

Instructions: To subtract on your jr.counter, you must push the beads down towards the reset zero position. (IT'S THE OPPOSITE OF COUNTING AND ADDING). Now you are taking away beads from the answer rod, not bringing them towards the answer rod.

Example
4 - 1

3 =

To subtract ① on your Jr. Counter, move the last lower bead down towards the zero, reset position.

Example
4 - 2

2 =

To subtract ② to your Jr. Counter move the two lowest beads down towards the ZERO, RESET POSITION.

To subtract ③ on your Jr. Counter, move the NEXT lower bead up towards the ANSWER-ROD so that it touches the second bead.

Example
4 - 3

1 =

To subtract ④ move the NEXT lower bead down towards the ZERO-RESET POSITION so that it IS AWAY FROM THE ANSWER BEAM.

Example
4 - 4

= 0

IT'S ALL the SAME

Remember, when subtracting you are moving beads away from the answer beam. Just move the number of beads that you are subtracting away from the answer beam. Just push the bead away from that answer rod to subtract.

Practice Skill 5 - Subtracting 0-4

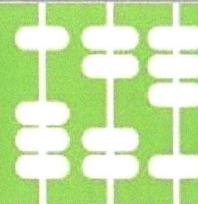

Directions: Complete the following subtraction calculations by moving the correct number of beads down and away from the answer-beam.

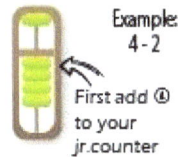

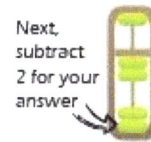

Example: 4 - 2
First add ④ to your jr.counter

Next, subtract 2 for your answer

2	1	2	2	4	4	3	3	4	3
1	0	2	0	0	1	1	3	2	2
1	......	......	......	......	......	......	......	......	......

1	2	2	1	0	3	3	1	1	2
2	......	......	......	......	......	......	......	......	......

Problem

Madam C. J. Walker had 3 bank accounts (from selling her hair products), and gave 1 away to The Tuskegee Institute. How many bank accounts did she have left?

Step 1: figure out what's being added or taken away in the problem

Step 2: write your number sentence to show what's being added or taken away

your number sentence

....

Step 3: write your answer

....

Practice Skill 5 - Subtracting 0-4

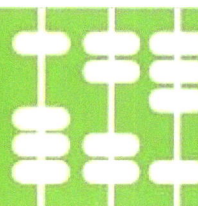

To subtract correctly on my jr.counter, I need to:
....
....
....

2	1	2	2	4	2	3	4	3	3
- 1	- 0	- 2	- 1	- 0	- 0	- 1	- 4	- 2	- 1
1	....	....	....	....	....	....	....	....	....

Problem

Imhotep designed 3 pyramids for King Tut and 2 for Nefertiti. How many more pyramids did Imhotep design in for King Tut than he did for Nefertiti?

Step 1:
figure out what's being added or taken away in the problem

Step 2:
write your number sentence to show what's being added or taken away

your number sentence

....

Step 3:
write your answer

....

Directions: Draw the number of legs on the insect that match the correct answer.

Example

2 + 0

2 + 2

3 + 1

1 + 2

0 + 4

4 - 3

Read more about the super heroes from your word problems

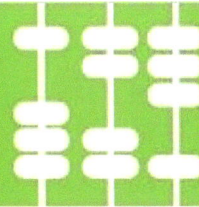

Mary Bowser

Mary Bowser: Move over K.C Undercover here is **ONE OF THE BRAVEST AMERICANS IN HISTORY:** Mary Bowser! Mary Bowser believed in equality and freedom.

She was super smart and especially clever. She was so smart that she worked for the American Government during the Civil War. The worst war ever. She disguised herself and tricked America's enemies into hiring her to work in their White House. And with her clever disguise she got valuable information which helped the Americans win the war. When the enemies finally realized her disguise she didn't just run away to safety, she first tried to burn down their White House.

Explain one thing you learned about Mary Bowser: ....
....

List two of her characteristics: ....
....

Why do you think Mary Bowser decided to spy? ....
....

Robert Smalls

Robert Smalls: This extremely smart and courageous man successfully freed himself, his family and many other enslave people from the plantations of human traffickers. He took over a naval boat, disguised himself as the captain and sailed himself and his family from the South to the free North. Later he successfully entered politics and became a congressman representing South Carolina.

Explain one thing you learned about Robert Smalls: ....
....

List two of his characteristics: ....
....

Why do you think Robert Smalls decided to take the naval ship? ....
....

Read more about the super heroes from your word problems

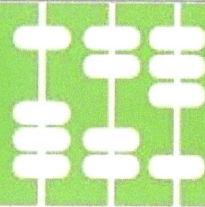

Harriet Tubman

She was a Civil War Super Hero. She had powers that made people around her brave. She faced dangerous and scary wilderness, usually by herself, to rescue people who had been kidnaped by evil human traffickers. She was also super smart. With no GPS she depended on the highly secretive Underground Railroad to stay safe. Like Mary Bowser, she served the US Army as a spy during the Civil War.

Explain one thing you learned about Harriet Tubman: ....
....

List two of her characteristics: ....
....

Why do you think Harriet returned to free people instead of staying safe?
....

Madam C. J. Walker

Madam C. J. Walker: You think Bill Gates was self made? Meet C.J., one of the richest most successful business people in America. Her curiosity and her desire to help people with their hair and beauty needs drove her to developing hair care products and cosmetics for African American women. She made her products by having experiments in her bathroom. She was so smart she figured out how to run her own company and became the first black American female millionaire! She named her company: Madame C. J. Walker Manufacturing, Co and was able to give thousands of people jobs.

If you were alive when Madam C. J Walker was alive, would you like to work in her company? ....
Why? ....

What do you think Madame C.J. Walker did with some of her wealth?
....
....

Would you buy any of Madame C.J. Walker's hair care products? ....
Why? ....

Read more about the super heroes from your word problems

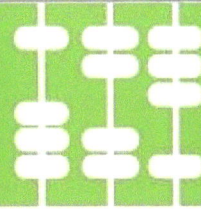

He was so brilliant that people called him the "God of Medicine." But his brilliance didn't stop there he was also a great mathematician, and a genius architect. He didn't design homes, he designed some of the greatest structures on the planet—Egyptian pyramids! He was just as creative and imaginative as he was smart. Actually, the design of the very first pyramid was his big idea.

What shapes are pyramids? ....
If you were to build a new structure what shape would you select?
....
....

What do you think Imhotep's childhood was like?
....
....

What kinds of things do think Imhotep cured, for him to get such a great title? ....
....

What are some things you have in common with Imhotep?
....
....

www.ingramcontent.com/pod-product-compliance
Lightning Source LLC
Chambersburg PA
CBHW041555040426
42447CB00002B/182